Un-

Black Widow Press is an imprint of Commonwealth Books, Inc., Boston, MA. Distributed to the trade by NBN (National Book Network) throughout North America, Canada, and the U.K. All Black Widow Press books are printed on acid-free paper, and glued into bindings. Black Widow Press and its logo are registered trademarks of Commonwealth Books, Inc.

Joseph S. Phillips and Susan J. Wood, Ph.D., Publishers
www.blackwidowpress.com

Cover Artwork: Swag (detail) by Linda Lynch, Pastel pigment on cotton paper, 30 x 44 inches, 2007
Cover design: Linda Lynch
Artwork, page 168: Little Karst Drawing by Linda Lynch, Pastel pigment on cotton paper, 60 x 44 inches, 2017
Book production: Kerrie L. Kemperman

ISBN-13: 978-0-9995803-7-0

Printed in the United States
10 9 8 7 6 5 4 3 2 1

Un-

Heller Levinson

BLACK
WIDOW
PRESS

unconscionable

5/1/10

UN

UNINHABITABLE

unbelievable
unfriend

underwear
undeserve

-veiled
unruly
unable

unrest

unnecessary
undeliverable
unbelievable
uncanny
unmoved
unloved

unduly

unconcerned
unlikely   unleash
unlearn   unilateral
        underpass

uncanny
underprivileged
underserved

understudy

uncharted understore

uncouth unqualified

unbelievable
underserving

uninformed

understanding understood

unsightly

unaccustomed

unlearn

understore

unreliable

unqualified

unable
excusable

unlikely   unplug

underscore

unsettle

unrelenting

uninational

uninterested
uncontaminated

understanding

unbecoming

uninterested

unqualified

— dulation

— deliverable

— welcome

circumferences cleansed,   inclined

toward rebound   (*from* "Rectilinear Limpidity")

for Linda Lynch

askew in vexative disarray

disqualified from the marching band

topsy-turvy trombone drool

reveille with ill-fitting trousers

reliability depends upon premature remorse

a bug in the hand beats a bite on the skin

tumbleweed   tactility   orthogonal

the one missing glove made for a cold hand

so much

so kind

so what

askew undergoes electroshock

clobber klatch catacomb crawdaddy

     covet castanet clutch

crunch

  c

     r

   u   m

b

        l y

     carousel chaos

forelimb fragmen tation

berserk blast bombast bludgeon

warp wobble bumble burp

wreck-burble shank scram

  Shazam Wham

do-se-doe

how ya feelin'?

better?

there ya go

in the pith of askew

      disquiet

          discord

               desuetude

dissolution deck

athwart   tumble-through

discharge

re

combine

combinatories ://: combustibles

        complementaries

the gun lay on the table the smile not far behind.

askew in operative distinction

grandiloquent   Cardinal   Stradivarius

            fantail flush filigree frost

→   at a glance

        up the sleeve

        off the cuff

        over the shoulder

        against the wall

        what's the point

There is no need to philosophize about language when language explains itself by showing itself.

in the pith of tenuous

t   e   m   p   o   r   a   l

t   i   m   e   r   i   t   y

t   r   e   m   u   l   o

u   s

tenebraed to tenuous

treacherous

tingle

tangle

thread

thorough fare

this

thus

then

now

when

where in the

way –

ward

is

to –

ward

rectilinear limpidity

chastened by aforethought the

circumferences cleansed,

                    inclined

toward rebound,

                    the putty

of play

from the scowl of a broken algorithm

dehiscence   ledger leak

fault line

a bleached orthodoxy wafts ~   ~   ~   ~

~   ~   ~

~   ~

breathless

indisputable

askew in formative rebuke

scullery   scallion crust   raillery on

the banks of perturbed promotional wheels

fustian fearsome clatter raw

crash crucible

crud-rusty

acclimatize crumble

curling backwater bushwhack bastions energized by

decidability formulas they grew mistaken

barrel pillage rake ravage

acerbate demolition grate gristle gruesome

bombs away

I am. this assertion pleases me to no end. that I emerge
from the threatening *LinguaQuake* tsunamis scuppering
foundations, shattering identities, an environment
totally unfriendly to a self stumbling to assemble, to
arrive comfortably situated among 'likenesses,' to find,
indeed, that I have a peer group, — the Un-identified.

where in the

vowel

is

velocity

the exploratory

resists

the

hortatory

askew over the rut

                        befall   fallen

                        upon

                        cover

                        crest

stumble

tumble crumble

akimbo

askance

                                        glance off

                peel ://: paste

                                      splinter

                pullulate

how much of

gather

in the

undo

postural spatial-seize

adhesive report

delirial abutments phrase a calisthenics devoted to

circumstance

in lieu of

         the partial

         the hidden

patrol ships off the coast

aliments in regurgitated depression

the clap to gather the entrecotes grass fed

pastorals still lovely after all these years

'drift ice' is slick slackens upon receipt of resistance

& you ask

why I like

country music

askew in disseminative fervor

abracadabra crunch quaquaversal quark

quicksilver gibbous grunge goblet gravitate

      queasy   lullaby   easy

lark spur roll undulate flow fold rip aberrate farfara

      frizzle flight flux

      flummox flotate feast found hound fount feral

      bestial leer

frunctorial fromage

fizzle-fraught

emission commission submission admission

      transmission permission

supple supplier no-denyer Dardenelle Dunkirk draconian loop-lie lob-toss trek curve carve crave legerdemain when-wren feign wane alterior domain supplicate restrain untrain encourage refrain speculate bombinate accelerate mush musket muster spirit the loop-loll lull-lapping lingual fricassee

Dear Jonathan,

Just initiating a new area stimulated by a discussion with Kurt DeVrese when he asked what does the Desert Sound like (me: lizard lapping, cacti slurping), — brought me to think about our language, .. what does p sound like, s, t, etc. so, attached is "Sonata in P," & will begin "Mass in S Minor" I'm thinking.

But behind these application-stabs is a broader picture & intention, i.e., to bring (or reclaim) topography, geology (i.e., as in "Karst," recently on alligatorzine.be), musical composition, lingualscape as landscape, etc.

Of course all this is Embodied in HT, but this is, as it were, the 'mathematical' proofs verifying the musicality, topology, of P. A flesh-out.

It was debated whether or not to employ musical notation in the piece but was decided not to, so as not to rein-in the reader who should feel free to interpret, to try differing speeds, rhythms, volumes, etc. I might try one sign just to signal possibilities, oh, I love it, THE P OPERA, 3 hours of performance devoted to P.

Sonata in P

(for Kurt Devrese

puffdaddy pencil point penitentiary perfidious prolix

puddle prank punk pucker

prick

pizzle

placate   placenta   parsimonious

puzzle

purl pearl pundit plank

press pontiff potential potentate plunk puncture prom-

ulgate propagate pest profit pubescent prong proof

p's & . . .   peas   *pizz er ia*

prime prolix ponder Pythagoras

persuasion   project   pause   purse   pursue

pump pomp parry pommel   pompom   parity

pungent post practical pincer pinch   p r a w n

pitch

parasol

plumb potential present pomegranate

perfidious peduncle predicate   perfect

                          propel

                    plumage

          perish

Mass in S Minor

solemnity   sear-solemn, >   s o a k

        suspend sully

               sanctimonious

        sermon

                        scare

                        suspect

                        suck

                        succubus

soar salty seal situate

             surround

             serpent

             seize

             squash

             squawk

             squeal

supplant

serendipitous sustenant succor source scintillate

        sumptuosity

                    sickness

suspirant succulent sensuous sincerity

                              soul

                  spirit

     sidereal

the tear within

transpierced   bellow

    thorn-rack   cavitous cobble

tumult-tumble   incinerate bearings

grip greased pell- mell wobble vertiginous gaga-stagger

            loss-loft

            ferocity-fade

            incurable crank

lump-laden

within the tear

glumblown   gearstrain

      plummetperil   perplexityplunge   parabolapinch

dicegrimygristlefold

caulkgraven

ravenrustle

crossgrain

                  roughagericketyranklerind

rust

bedlam

in the stricken of bugle brawn

coll   apse

     i

    bles

tear like anfractuous thirst

thrive-shrunk   decibel-pound

    twine-rot   scorbutic-squirt

        scrounge-scutter

        grunge-vine

        gristle-tart

     quoit—quarter—quarantine

calculus

cordillera crunch

encaustic intermidget rasp rust ridge rangy

rank

scurrilous

scrape

<< what does the proof improve >>

in the nook of lime

from blear-beat

>   to the blear-beat frazzle frills of a condemned

analytic

artichoke heart

cadaver suds

ruminations upon the present & future in elapsed time

digital resolve lacks confusion

spites uninvited crossovers

unobligated currents

a helter skelter sanity conniving for appointment

in the pith of improve

constitute   construct

        craft

where in improve is progress

build upon

is the built-upon fused into the newly built

does the improved require approval

in the pith of embark

flawless   stripped clean

                bone forward

where in the

embark

is

meander

lawless rout

reckless encounter

skinning the erstwhile   nobility shorn

                wreck reckless   bluster estuarial

facsimile bleed   burnish glide   hygiene disarray

loll lollipop languorous linger lounge

                loafe lean

        askew   lanky

        dismount

                        heels to the

East

uneven

quaint

wacky   quaky   quack

quirk

The escape velocity of earth is 225,000 mph.

What is the escape velocity of conditioning?

'''

what entitles us to colonize other planets when we are

incapable of caretaking our own?

in the pith of still

t   h   I   s

        o   n

            l

                        y

the ball dribbles into the street. a virile dribble. plenty
of airtosterone. vehicles unamused. persons non plus.
against the curb the ball slows. unbounces. rolls to a
grate. stills.

the dribble still in the ball.

still.

in the pith of remark

Beckett has said: "Every word is like an unnecessary stain on the silence and nothingness."

Dear reader: please don't permit Becketts' remark (his *words*, after all) to inhibit you from commenting upon "in the pith of remark." any blemish outbreak will quickly retreat before the cleansing rays of illumination.

: the more precision deposited at the foot of the mysterious the more mysterious the mystery becomes :

in the pith of inexplicable

tongue-tied   trussed

                                        choice   prime

        abeyance   vexative

    in the distil of evaporative

        catch

        glint-glance

        gristle

        glisten

on the occasion of strip-husking,

wild bark celebrates

        dithyrambic dislodge

studying hard for finals the noise abates

consider salt water as lodging

in the exhaust of askew

disarray   retch recitative

                                            wrack wreckage

                                            wrung-wring

apostles no longer saturated but appealing

crevices gasp for wall for the monumental   the

    sturdiness that

rebukes that

staves involuntary ambush   . . .

. . . .

outskirted by the debris of a

hurting madrigal

illogic inclines

where in the

embrace

is the

unfold

in Spring, the finch sports its yellow . . ~

~   ~

Gustaf Sobin: "Stillness is the inconceivable velocity of our flesh, thinking in the same space-cadence as the universe."

Stillness is the universe inward-ed, emptied of spiral,
magnetization, tide, . . . definition.
Stillness is the art of disappearance

the involute convoluted

of course considerations matter if not merely a matter of bending binding time that corollary of endless function continuity's doppelganger fizzling with the introduction of design

of course then only & only then with moxie due diligence & the dazzling d's among the cherries the wood thrush the bumble bees by the by bumptious not only but merely with flex flux flattery a fraternity of matrixes along the diphthong curious the flock the insect the swarm

of course not only a big huge between the haves & nots the clear perfect fouled by blemish by the underwhelm accumulation requires put throughs prioritizations justifications juries spooled through private through lark "I" lagoons theirs is theirs yours an is not the capsize unremarkable so far
down below

trundle evaporate

(for Linda Lynch

mullet-marl   mallet-maul   membranous makeover

windage-skid

ferrule-scrape

spur parade

the days grow hot O' Babylon

going forth — solitude-stitched   bewilder-peppered

uncertainty-braced . . . spine spindling — with unravel

as precondition you await the debrief, soreness stippled,

sanity skinned, slices congregate to sustain appetite, the

uncontrollable no longer convicted but convincing,

pouched in reticulum a conversation of sorts, a loin

suspicion, . . . crank equivalence fumigates a bedlam of

soiled ocelots, concubines pillage for stall, trepidation

underscores the pause, not unlike a walk relearned,

spool-twists refute gravitational bias, leech to an arboreal

numerology, this is not recreational silence, nor

ceremonial ostentation, . . .

where in the

wound

is

beseech

terminals for perplexity repair, mallet wardens mush

tremolo, far off a buzzard, a space for carpentry, the

noise of an earring falling, errant accumulates, sidereal

salutation, stropping the dirge with open fire &

triumphalism,

looping a lapsed archaic,

the grasp

anything

but final

>> nothing: the not that nots <<

you too this only this indication slight slathered with

bulbosity bared to the bone only so much one can make

of this who would want to

clearly a realm apart distant far off far from the chatter

the clatter of disengenuity joint relief   jealous husbands

jury duty   you want

out   sign

here

you go first you did alleviation was a state of mind

mindfully you mined mine mind muck meretricious

masterful moxie most parentheses stay clear of the collar

Otherwise what would be the point days could go by

no matter no what like this pertinence persists until

reconstitution redirects achieves constructs supports to

keep the fade at bay likewise provide relief if only but

hardly

Otherwise who would want what incentive to an

undertaking fouled

with remiss   hypertension   toilsome format

malodorous

the dream of many the reach extending extensive so far

high far out outreaches to try for worthy goals (grab

obtain possess) pocked with remission perilous scant

resource shoddily attacks from all sides possibilities exit

strategies shrunk shrink shrank the gloom all entirely yet

but for

in the pith of vestige

earth rumble   ramifi

cation   hurdle hop

            drowse-alert

the let that lets go   upcharge →

aboriginal arrowhead: a depth deposit

a retrieval-twined extrusion   nudge

toward

in the swell of swollen liquidity → *flare*

how much of

remains

is contained

quarry contained: tricked to the confines of narrow

corridors, where hunter elates & prey stiffens

aboriginal arrowhead: the left behind, the

newly renewed

where in the

contained

is the

voluble

the

consideration . . .

utterances —

bemired

crawling

clawing

in the pith of drift

wander   mosey   circumambulate

  delect   grace notes

span   to arrive at arrival

(vestige: a drift appearing

time-churned   mud-drudge silkily

sulked   soused   sultry with

deviation)

borealis-swirl   sizzle broth

      bumptious boomerang

sluice glide   unhobbling the aids of a

rent asperity the burgeon-forth trigger-gloam glides the

glide fantastic

aspirates

if only somehow sometimes clearly things were different crepuscular crepuscular differing a trial of nations trail overwhelm overshadow stalwart surprises the efforts behind making shaping bringing to bear moribund elusive pulsative enhance flame fuel fume fire bulwark bastion bombinate bazaar bizarre a stretch a fade of sorts

nests   one twig at a time

the go-between not unseemly but. unlike. unlike the

heretofore. which prioritizes. mingling prioritization

with a priori. the truths as if sometimes somewhere

somehow the glide accumulates. announces. that way.

manner. of making. putting pulling forth.

punctuation as funereally inspired. motif. nightcaps.

mudflaps. wardens of. dispatch. do se do's. daresay.

pirates rank privilege as booty biased. the stuff of

things.

    digging.

    always.

    however.

dread as euphemistic misdemeanor

scant raucous quark

lodging dislodged

mad ice counterattacks scurrilous batten

       form cube, form chilagon, form chrysanthemum,

       chartreuse, mushroom, … smirk

dreams seldom outlast the flavor of ice cream

upright is no longer feasible

tisket   tasket   belay the yellow basket

everybody has a 'Lester' story

dark to bark across

elongative fealty   spatial

bruise   caliper crunch

  c a l i b r a t i o n

distance: a series of sums

dark: intumescence

the lute arks splashes tropical

discharges . . . confides

a legato loses its way

in the ache of writhe

fester   torque   twist

                tether tangle

in the pith of tenuous

apostrophe flail   ribbon scraggle

        m   i   r   e

falter   rub unbraid   metrical dissolve

mallet puncture

pustule puss

malignancy

the cage was flexible but non-

itinerant

the ruling class was all

a' jitters

under the guise of merriment

profound flounder The Portrait:

no point in using red when

only black will do

mulling umber

mewling amber

vicissitudes over stone

dirty underwear requires washing

the washing machine: a paen to pattern

Pattern: the underlying underbelly

where in the

hollow

are the

outskirts

peeling to margins →. . . a

frozen choir

fleshing over cornerstones

ampoules deliberating

the blue armchair exudes blue as well as

comfort.

the heretics fled. the bushes filled with spies. the

weather puckered.

the blue armchair oozes leisure. solace. the blue of the

armchair swells. asserts itself as blue. swells with

invitation.

the blue armchair stuttering in

complexity wraps itself in mood.

blue mood.

the blue armchair concerned about acquiring

complacency fictionalizes crimson.

the blue armchair was nothing if not a blue armchair.

the blue armchair was often uncompanionable. often uncomfortable with occupation. much of the time the blue armchair was defined by dissatisfaction.

when the blue armchair was feeling unsociable, it was neither a hindrance nor a deprivation. it did, however, require accommodation.

such an 'accommodation' — for the blue armchair, plunged into consternation, sunk into a deep funk — was often provided. by, in the evening, a weighty posterior sinking into the fabric & distributing the disturbed muddle.

in the pith of elongative

sea creatures   Mariana Trench

                Pinocchio

rattling the perpendicular parallel prolix

                                  tropistic forethought

                                      compressed concinnity

where in the

elongative

is

suspension

[to irk   [to irk into stroll

      strand percolative

      ribbon wave

      wand wisteria

how much of

distance

is

separation

:: do Giacometti's walking figures, in their elongated

sequestration, their inclined ambulation, suggest a

distance to 'nowhere' . . . ? if 'anywhere' is merely an

arbitrary devisement of points encased by the Big

Empty, what, then, is distance but vacuous measure-

ment, empty illusion, . . . abyssal reek ::

how much of

elongation

is

transmission

mutables meshed evanescent

~ ~ ~ ~

Giaco Considered:

"He began to create figures that were increasingly elon-

gated, emphasizing their solitary nature and a sense of

isolation." (Commentary at Guggenheim Exhibition)

The above is a common response to Giaco's figurations & is based upon endowing them with philosophical intent rather than understanding they outcrop from the artist's struggle to see. Giaco was obsessed with getting to the truth of the model. He was not interested in expressing his 'feelings' but in embracing verity. Figures not to be viewed as 'emaciated,' but as compressed, squeezed forth – like toothpaste – with the exhortation to manifest, to appear, . . . massaging into shape an insight extrusion. The elongation is the outcome of the pursuit. He was not interested in *expressing* but in *knowing* – "At root I work only for myself, striving to know what I'm seeing." – Giacometti

Giaco's Walking Figures

are sternly directional. They are saturated with intent.

They appear determined, like they are headed

somewhere, destination bound. & yet, undermining

this rock-solid intentionality, one feels a swamp of

emptiness, a humongous yawp of void.

That Giaco could achieve this antipodal tension is

remarkable: the human animal purposeful to no

purpose.

Weather as Pleasantry

The contemporary city dweller's closest approximation
to the natural world is most likely weather, — an
elemental force that in the past would inspire both fear
& reverence.

Now suffering tyrannical media homogenization, this
last vestige of vitalism is being harnessed into domesti-
city, formatted for maximum sanitation, produced to
purr like a pet cat, caged for spectacle, suburbanized
into just another everyday pleasantry.

The most pernicious outcome from this Weather
Emasculation is having our feelings about the weather
dictated to. In what has become a cult of Weather
Morality, we are told that sunny days are good, rainy
days bad, clouds are troublesome, snow is hazardous,

extreme conditions are voyeuristically exciting &, if we stay tuned, live coverage will transport these adrenaline delectables to our feasting table.

The sheer arrogance of weathermen to presume what is 'good' or 'bad' for us is deeply disturbing.

Many persons enjoy the rain, enjoy contrasts, even relish — *stormy weather.* Whatever became of the beloved Parisian Gris, of the joy of being beside a blazing fire with a loved one while a storm whips your mountain hut.

Who are these hierarchical dogmatists who *rate* the weather for us, — who declare a *pick* of the week; who have erected a schemata for 'the top five days of the month'?

They are corporate automatons governing/shaping/ manipulating our thinking for us. Or, perhaps more accurately, they *do* our thinking for us.

They comprise The Great Global Meltdown of Individualism.

The Cowardly Non-Thinking New World.

hover like prodigious volumes trans

lucing

sluice-floes loft lumbrous

propel altitudinous

scant friction ~ ~

where in the

distance

is

access   accumulation   ingredient

the strap-sprung ether-bounce intertangle

the species of spatial defiance

the trapdoor

of suction

just suppose, thought the armchair, if I could honor my aversions, if, say, repulsed by a certain person, I could summon the power to reject them, to be able, as soon as a revolting posterior posted upon my comfort station, to eject them into the atmosphere, send them hiking.

alternatively, Blue mused over an agreeable perhaps deliciously succulent posterior, . . . alluring, temptious, provocative. Such a presentation would reverse the impulse to repel with the desire to compel: compel to prolong, to bask in, to become a part of, join, ... fuse, to sensuously soak, swallow, to glow in the glissades of amour. Would incite the urge to possess rather than dismiss.

These bipolar considerations did not stress Blue.

S/he embraced supple.

in the pith of void

vac   an   cy

    absen   tee   ism

       grid-gap

churl maw

drain   unrudder, . . . chalky

    vortex vacuum

'asunder' the implausible broker

intersectional delete

complexity deplete

diurnal vitiate

shutter subtract platter evaporate

the poise of pose wobbles

              , ponders an unearned intensity

derelict wrung-wring

cataract fade

soured ricochet

spatial strangulate

in the crib of

expired bedlam

a

gaze

slackens

Void

density's

objection

void like antediluvian misfit

harried   hallowed   hollow

                        hoist

                        howl

vowels unsteady – wobble prone,

rickety

                        plunge drumfire reed spit

                        nostrum slurp flare

no money down

weed wallopers credit anticipation as the pledge of

choice

the whores in Modesto have no teeth

where in

deterioration

is

sullen

askew in variant disposition

tilt kilter cutter cloy   concavity

     cloven-foot   clunker

        skid trip falter flaw

        'Topsy' (tom toms)

deprivation: depravity primed

wobble wrangle

angle

tangle

plump in the perihelion palaver heist

antigodlin pock

Giacometti's Gaze

> "What made the difference between a dead man
> and the person was the gaze."[1] – Giacometti

For Giacometti, verity dwelled in the gaze. If we honor
his assertions, truth is what he sought from art. As he
puts it:

> This is what stimulates me, as if one should at
> least get to the point of understanding the secret
> of life. I know it is utterly impossible for me to
> model, paint, or draw a head for instance, as I see
> it, yet this is the one thing I am trying to do.[2]

He further adds: "New Hebrides sculpture is true, and
more true, because it has a gaze." What sort of

écrits is an abbreviation for *Alberto Giacometti: écrits,* edited by Michel Leiris and
Jacques Dupin, Paris, Hermann 1990.
[1] Interview by Charbonnier, 1951, .loc. cit. pp. 162-3 (*écrits*, p.243-4).
[2] Answer to Peter Selz, loc. cit. (*écrits*, p. 84)

knowledge, then, can be gathered from the gaze, & in what capacity might it enable us to "know the secret of life?"

It will not be the purview of this exploration to comment on the psychological, inter-subjective meaning that the 'gaze' had for Giacometti. Rather, through his pedestalizing the 'gaze' as an epistemological nugget, we will seek to discover what the gaze might mean to us. Where in the gaze is the 'secret of life.'

How does the gaze differ from the look, the peer, the regard, the delve-immerse/into[3] or what Van Gogh called "watching?"[4] To give 'gaze' as wide a berth as possible, gaze will be viewed as inclusive of the above terms or others that satisfy the criteria of any prolonged

---

[3] see *Wrack Lariat* (Black Widow Press, 2015) p. 205.

[4] On hearing music, Vincent said: "I should be *watching* (Italics mine) the musicians rather than listening." Ibid., p. 217.

& intense seeing whose intention is to *peer-into* with an eye toward extraction.

What is it exactly that we are hoping to extract? It is the essential beingness of what is on view, its quintessential quiddity. The 'that' which is *before* one, which presents itself as *appearance*.

Today, the entire sensory realm has been hijacked by what Frederick Jameson terms the "logic of late capital-ism." Our visual world is glutted with stimulation, assaulted with an unceasing barrage of images. Com-merce has identified the eye as the ultimate consumer & has targeted it accordingly. The eye, coerced to the gallows of expenditure, is voided of gaze. When not 'under attack,' the eye is entrained into instrumentality by tracking the useful. It is a primary physiological component of driving one's vehicle to the shopping mall where it can follow the purposeful cues at Stop & Shop, i.e., aisle 5 for soap, aisle 2 for cereal. The eye no longer *seeks* but *computes*.

The gaze, in contrast, is flotational, disallocational, non-mechanistic, anti-sequential, non-transactional, attenuative, nuanced, & fluid — the gaze euphorizes to the rhythmic flux of Bergsonian duration.[5]

Key interrelated components of the gaze are:
1. Suspension 2. Absence 3. the Peer

To mobilize the model[6] to come forth, one must disengage oneself from the temporal, one must 'stand still like the hummingbird.'[7] Just as human movement in the forest will cause animals to scatter, so the model may be

---

[5] Referring here to the destruction of clock time; the idea that the time of physics is merely derived.

[6] The term 'model,' both personal & impersonal, will apply to the 'what' being gazed upon.

[7] Henry Miller's book of that name.

fragile & elusive, reluctant to appear unless secure of a non-threatening & appreciative clearance. The viewer must attain a state of suspension,[8] must ready the perceptual pores for complete receptivity. This state of complete openness is achieved by *absenting* all considerations, banishing all distractions, obstacles, & blockages. Perhaps most difficult of all, the 'self' must dissolve, must melt into a reservoir of communality, must *delve-immerse/into* the Other. When such conditions apply, the model will generate activity, will vibrate with appeal, will become succulent with invitation. The unremitting drift of additional magnetically accumulative phenomena in differing articulations requires the gazer to keep peeling away the facets to insure complementary densification.

---

[8] Note the word 'suspense' lurking in 'suspension.'

The gaze is more than mere reception. Prolonged deep-seeing releases the see(e)r & model from the situated[9] as they fuse to a current charged with shimmer, with diffuse & formulation, new livelinesses spawn, unlikely shapes appear, the trans-retinal whorl-blends with the strictly perceptive, dimension oscillates, horizon flutters, optical fireworks bedizen.

This coupling, this interosculative *other*-ling, constitutes the *magni*-ficence of the gaze.

Less dialogue, than

con-gress.

---

[9] The 'situated' refers to our social/acculturated world a-soot with contextualization, reference, & signification.

in the pith of distill

aeration   roam-attar

g   a   t   h   e   r

r   e   l   e   a   s   e

g   a   t   h   e

r

r   o   a

m

how much of

gaze

is

distillation

crumbs. crumbs cause me distemper. they are the
refuse of refusal. the refusal to consider. the other.
what an other might find objectionable. insupportable.
insufferable. probably a major cause for my discomfort
at being in this household. with inconsiderate persons.
insufferable. well, the wife is not so bad. she's not
prone to crumb me. but then, she rarely sits upon me.
at least, not with anything resembling regularity. He, on
the other hand, & maybe it's a gender thing, is
predictable & insufferable. did I use that term before?
insufferable? perhaps a queer word for an armchair to
articulate given that an armchair, myself in this case, is
manufactured for sitting. yet, there is sitting & then
there is sitting. or should I say, plopping. plopping is
formless. lacks class. gracefulness. yes, the he of the
household is a plopper. bona fide.

askew in fugitive distillation

crib-strain   pot-stain

      mulberry-mush

      ferry-hop

      furlough

wanderlust squeezed of frequency

gateways pucker insouciant while

      armies unsilenced by night squiggle perturbative

mandolin matrix

a passion for the history of the nail clipper overtakes

philosophy departments

so many ways

to cleat

where in the

enterprise

is

congestion

Shadow Translate

hierophant fawn   equipollent

rub-out

                 soothsay

                 sundry

                 sug-gest

arrear

annotate

anneal

                 a departure

                              yet

dependent

                 part of

                              yet

separate

                 circumstantial

                 split

alternating

off shoot

Dialogics: **The Dialogics are ongoing conversations between Will Alexander & Heller Levinson. They began in 2001 in Los Angeles over beer & burgers at "The Saloon" on Pico Boulevard. Below is a sampling of recent exchanges.**

H: I'm intently interested in learning to see better (we should asterisk 'learning' as a subject to return to; to consider how to acquire true learning as opposed to the institutionally dished-out). While working with Van Gogh, I feel I received valuable instruction in the art of seeing. Reading letter #340 to Theo where Vincent describes what he 'saw' as he rode into the village, smote me with the realization that I was a perceptual amateur. Yet, understanding my visual impoverishment is what inspired me to achieve more perceptual adeptness.

This confession of my own inadequacy is served up to indicate what opportunities our limitations provide us in the way of being-in-the-world creatively. Working to enhance one's capabilities lavishes continuously delirial stimulation totally freed from the capitalist consumption matrix.

Don't you feel the dissemination, the instruction, in this type of 'news' could challenge the oligarchical technological tyranny?

Would we be shut down like the journalists in Myanmar? Or would what we consider to be a Medicinal Revolution simply evaporate as a non-threat, incapable of wrenching the teething-toy-gadgets away from the screen-possessed?

W: What you propose is the active writhing of conscious being. Active being is not unlike the vivacity of a mongoose that telepathically senses menace. It is by mining the essence of this aforesaid telepathy that one begins to espy unanswered planes where sensitivity takes on an invisible grammar. This is where the soul transcribes itself and begins unfolding itself to itself. This is where information organically ignites as a flare of wisdom, as triangulated gulls wafting into darkness.

To the modern sensibility information no longer insists on curvature, on the beauty of seeming irregularity. Instead, it functions via scattered remarks, via the agglutenation of symbols transposed so as to square with lineal examination and secular conclusion. Via heightened clauses of the mind one leaves the glaze that appends superficial dazzling, a dazzling that qualifies as law clerk, as CEO of the motor division, thus one is scripted to fit into a-priori normalization.

Such a level of consciousness remains noise ridden, optical, cherished as mechanical property. As for the mongoose and its skill, there remains no ability to track its intelligence of aether. The mongoose mind not unlike an antidote to gross manifestation. I am thinking along the lines of Egyptian education and its opening to the soul. Its teachers or guides were entitled Hersethas. For instance, if one studied geography or mathematics, it was not only the technical properties of these subjects but an exercise of being. One was not subjected to the totalizing mirage of material acquisition. Instead one was guided by an alchemical subtext so that one could first see and then experience realias that were not apparent.

Being educated at Luxor was not equivalent to say, the confines of UCLA or the University of Chicago. There was the burning grace of the mind, that spiraled as diamonds into the uranian. As for modern apprehension of such experience none can possibly apply. The texts, the quizzes of modern conditioning leaves us woefully unprepared for understanding the endless wastes of the cosmos. The latter being sans the visibility such as targeted journalists in Myanmar, all the while being completely invisible to common media gluttons as they swarm the continents teeming as they do via literal converse.

Superficially things seem not to be moved, but in terms of deeper movement, blizzards of consciousness affect not only our present hesitations, but also signal understanding that intensity exists beyond the skills that beset the private possessor of material goods and services.

H: Mongoose Shuffle

bulked by the plush of

mongoose, claused to the genus Herpestidae, to

the glory of an archaic electrical discharge remote from

noematic narcolepts, parliamentary

pundits, sclerotic scribes, I

of flesh & non-flesh, paste wing to fin, viper tongue to

tiger claw, spiral through the char of

anemic nations, alert, ever tenacious, dodging their

venoms, their spit redundancies, their

acidic recidivism, . . . intent, charged, detuning to the

key of paradox, registered to a higher aura, one cannot

withstand

puny binary scribble, cribbed psychic contaminations

deliberate by

design, faulty by

contagion, in conjunction with haruspex vault &

viola tremble, paired with an acute arrhythmia, I

somersault through

vacancies, to opalescent-combed silences, to errancies

unfrequented by nomenclature,

pulsating to a battery of toms toms aloof in their

unearth, careless of crease, indisposed to

surreption, both tooth fairy & isosceles

triangle, furtive & outspoken, loosed from a Chinese

junket & bobbing

with cattail, on my breath floats a

troubled mandolin strumming *Arboreal Romance,*

coming

from cloud, no longer walking,

I shuffle

both

inconspicuous

&

unanimous

H: Two twentieth century philosophers — Sartre & Levinas — holding oppositional views on the role of the Other gives one pause.

Sartre saw the other as a threat, a hostile, a presence whose function was to subvert one's freedom. The Other's gaze was a beam for petrification.

Alternatively, Levinas views the Other as a gateway to infinity, an opportunity to transcend objectification.

Why are these formulations so strictly exclusive? Why is there no consideration of a subject's agency to choose their own interpretation of the other. Why cannot a person see differing persons in differing lights? Subjects are not uniform, neither are Others. Why is there no suggestion of consciousness's elasticity to freely control how the Other manifests.

Certain persons might be vulnerable to Sartre's notion of the other as a 'fixative,' while others could remain immune.

I posit that the commercial element is largely responsible for these prioritized, one-sided, exclusionary, rigid systems.

These are professional philosophers we are talking about. They make their living teaching what other philosophers had to say while at the same time trying to establish a legacy by trotting out a fresh point of view. Building a philosophical edifice requires piling bricks of logic on top of one another along with persuasive refutations of other philosophies to lay claim to the validity of one's own.

Socrates, a non-professional, was put to death for philosophizing. He had no system, but he did have the gift of ignorance.

Do you share my notion that a New Philosopher must be born? Free from the constraints of commercial enterprise?

W: Education has instilled a somber lessened lucidity. Philosophy in this key being nothing other than rigidified calisthenics. An overview of the world via arcane rigidity, via its splintering of angle, via argument and the classification of systems. Each thinker reveals to the world a solemn trespasser's law, that he is being invaded by an infected overlay of thought, by the infected jaundice that convinces one's lesser ability to be. In spite of discussion concerning philosophical otherness the moon has been brought to Earth symbolic of a moribund psycho-physiological state with its inability to transmute. Where are the icebergs, where are the lions, where exists the crowning flame of nature? Thus, a terrible incompleteness persists. For prior generations nature seemed to be the deepest well of study.

The Occident, with its welter of phantoms can never illumine its fatal insistence concerning the sustenance of separation and conflict as a means to revelation. Everyday of every moment of Kant's or Hegel's existence the blood of an Indian was unlawfully spilled. So how could they argue from principled moral height. Having just witnessed Francisco Toledo's mesmeric print on the trans-Atlantic Middle Passage it impresses on me its subtext of dates that implicates a European moral curse. It remains brazen arrogance to line up souls in order to sell them having already cast them into the abyss all the while systematizing higher systems of mind. To this degree they broker with the abyss, they wake to the degree that we enter into psycho-physical cul de sacs that we then feed our own minds. Being one of 40 billion planets in the Milky Way alone how can we be reduced a portion of our psycho-reductive brethren who argue in plain view about the need to shout from a roof spiked with armed barriers.

Give me medicine for the soul. Give me the focus and strength to focus and absorb the other. It is according to the latter tenor that I become conversant with my own shadow, so that my statement to the world fails to empower conquest and argument. In this sense thought can become more analogous to organic independence, not unlike intense rogue planets emitting rays from their poles sans a rational solar family. In this sense one's mind needs be proto to a future not presently projected. A future not contained as cosmological utopia, but one that transmutes annihilation into unforeseen cellular irradiation.

Some new considerations:

Philosophy has entered the plane of heightened diversion. It has crossed into individual diversion. It has fostered an exclusionary enterprise where the figment postures as incremental imperator. Personal argument prevails. A reductive substantive transpires. The Individual is allowed to mock existence with what he or she considers a revelatory whim. This amounts to none other than concussion ethics, where a concussive glare parses the immeasurable into emboldened figments, into gestures of dire substantives.

W: Accosted by a tornado of cul de sacs, there persists a curious poison in the atmosphere. An incalculable blindness that rises and gestates as stagnation as daily kinetic. In this sense the populace is not unlike the waking dead who solemnly scale tedium never knowing when their last occurrence will transpire. As for the graph of blindness there exists a literal syncopation of lack. All the while the icebergs swelter, the moon as a dis-inhabited hull implies a zodiac that fails to shift signals to itself. At present, a non-aligned populace exists via gullible toxicity. Individual consumption takes on ritual significance for those who are solemnly brewed by damnation. Reality has become a deflated zoo of violence, with the only procrastination being one of who and what will be slaughtered. This being the subtended realia of the individual bourgeois who extends his dearth into an ersatz archaeology near the end of life as its commonly accepted as known.

As the void burns it listens to itself, by emitting signals by equating differing circumstance, priorities, and endings for say, Mayans, and Romans and now with the human species now entering impalatable arrhythmia of

climatic instability, of in-sustainable graft and degrada-
tion it seems the void is not self-summoning an analytic
property, but one of lasting problematic consequence.

How does mythology balance the overwhelming nature
of such consequence? How do prior chronicles condone
or assuage the abyss?

With all of the above would you say that the collective
now sails on a precarious raft of mercury?

H: Indeed, the poison fumes are propagating & deeply
saturant, . . . the apocalypse near at hand. (Symbolic
that I am penning this on 9/11 ?).

I would say that a raft, by definition, is precarious &
that the collective flotation device we are now upon is
suffering from rotting timber, fraying rope, . . . unplug-
gable leakage.

If one accepts that our species is approaching extinction,
that this time in history is exceptional, then prior
mythologies do not apply. Mythology functions to
insure continuity & to explain the inexplicable. When
confronted with Nullity, its usefulness expires.

What then?

We needn't trot out the by-now-familiar list of catastrophes that probability theory assures us will one day do us in, i.e., the ecological crisis, the proliferation of nuclear arms, etc., the evidence is in. The prevailing advice about how to live in what is fashionably called a 'post-human' world is generally scripted by the institutionally-obligated even as they pose as radical thinkers. Is not the very term 'post-human' curious? When did we ever arrive at a 'human' world? An institutional thinker such as Marc Augé in his book, *The Future*, bets on the future by proposing an "Educational Utopia." This is both naively fanciful & thoroughly impractical from every angle. First off, as Augé envisions this utopia, it would be impossible to finance. Secondly, for a sociologist, it is a gross miscalculation of human nature: people do not seek more or better education, they seek more *things*. Instruction in the art of Acquisition, however, would be sure to fire-up interest. But because he (we are just citing Augé here, who is merely one example) is a Director of Studies at a Paris University, he is compelled to provide a solution, no matter how flimsy, just to secure his job along with the possibility to publish more books. Imagine a University Employee finalizing his analytical study of today's societal condition with the admonition:

"In light of the above bleak analysis, I would recommend plenty of sex and alcohol."

It would be 'lights-out.'

Same for the politicians. They will not effect change for they are required to *appeal.* & what appeals to the collective is what will annihilate the collective because it is unsustainable.

Case in point: you want to go green & feel good about yourself in India you go buy an electric car. Trouble is the electric grid which powers your electric car is, in turn, being energized by coal production which has as severe climactic consequences as carbon monoxide emissions.

We cannot turn to those who have a stake in the game. They are *spoken for.*

Post-Holocaust, writers & artists were concerned how art could have any meaning or merit.

Pre-Termination, we could ask ourselves the same thing. Why write at all? Why go on? Well, this is where things get interesting. As you eloquently phrased it: "As the void burns it listens to itself, by emitting signals . . . it seems the void is not self-summoning an analytic property, but one of lasting problematic consequence."

What a wonderful time in world history to be an artist! At the very brink, having the opportunity to probe into Void Problematics, not like Beckett & Sartre with their aperitifs before them at the Café Flore, not with alienation & the abyss swirling in the abstraction of Gauloises smoke, but here, now, upon us, Void as The Intimate Neighbor, in your face, calling all artists to arms, this which is a thoroughly impractical address, void of remuneration, to be yet stirring, writhing in penumbra, capable of adventuring with this investigation at the very precipice of our species, what more can one ask for?

At the same time, I would recommend lots of sex & alcohol.

W: Billions and billions being molten with aphasia, disinterred, poltergeists, opinionated mongrels, trained via complicity with their own deracination. In this sense daily life remains concussive with strain, with hallucinating embers scattered along one's psychic route. Should one conclude upon quantification as meaning, one's density then seems to procure failure. The question arises, how does one face hordes of the hallucinated on a daily scale, via confronting, via the elusive, or via one's own circulation as being utterly other?

H: Having just addressed Termination, I suppose it is appropriate to now address the Walking-Terminated. Nowhere near as exciting, I assure you.

How to deal? I could reply with what is now becoming a mantra: more sex & alcohol. But that would be to renounce other possibilities. I feel confrontation should be employed at every opportunity, — readings, teachings, discussions, whenever possible to awaken consciousness. Also, at a strictly personal level, if a person sits down next to you on a train & continues talking loudly into their cell phone, definitely say something, definitely defend the ever-disappearing notion of civility, of mutual respect for another person's space & right not to be invaded by noxious blather.

Of course cherish one's own circulation, one's otherness. Be grateful that, as a profound artist, you have ready sources of nutrition available. Also important to keep in mind is that probably all our Artistic Mentors suffered, to some degree, feelings of estrangement. It comes with the territory. Like splinters for a carpenter, or bunions for a ballerina. Distance from the transactional modality is required for insight development.

Pragmatically, there are definite palliatives. In my own case, although I loved NYC, I couldn't stand seeing everyone enslaved to their phones. I sought solace with what I called a therapy-based investment strategy: I would put dollars into Apple, Verizon, AT&T, Samsung, then, when confronted with the omnipresent screen-slaves, I could console myself that while they de-humanized, I grew wealthier. Finally, although my investment strategy was helpful, I ultimately had to flee the city. Even if it means a longer commute to work, I would recommend living in less populated areas. Also helpful is spending more time with animals, pets or otherwise. Cross-species Hinging offers a plethora of opportunities for approaching Otherly Infinitudes.

where is the

digital

without

digits

how much of

intimacy

is

nuance

in the pith of nymphéas

(after the Musée Marmottan 10/2/18

sumptuosity   sure-ness   allure

    assuage   sloe   slough   sear

s   u   c   c   u   m   b

   flotation madrigal burgeon briar

      s   s   s   er

        un

            du

                late

tremor

entwine

ensign

sanc   ti   mon   i ous

in the breath-heave whorl of a suspended exuberance

lyre-loft perspicuity prolong

pearl azure

azurlite

where in the

frost

is

nymphéas

sage   licorice   lush

l   a   n   g   o   u   s   t   i   n   e

lustral-loll

g o u r m a n d e r i e

rowl overture

moss mist-moisten

con   cor   da

            nce

d   r   i

  f   t

trowel

trawl

drawl

t r e m o l o

seep

slather

slumber

meander

mur   mur   mural

cerule murmur orange viscous

slate   zephyr-flush

svelte savour

in the lunge of langour

this

bell　i　　　cos　　i　　ty

otherwise one could go on *if it werent for* thinking

interminable that there was nothing but   which is to say

the only way things go continue roll on roll on is in

conformity with abiding by the rules of buddy form

measurement logic-based facts management assesses

salutations surely the thing of it is another way of saying

this is it seems clear from the above passage formalism of

the matter as far as that goes stunning sort of furniture

holds things up that is which is to say insure continuity

support for those less fortunate under lower auspicious

circumstances characters nonetheless dependability

durable endure secure lecture to count counting upon

accountability the gross add-up depending upon

arrangement I am to you as you are to me accruing

structure bone wardens delight most everything but for

the good will provide most everything happiness to all

bear the brunt grant the stamp authentic rant rarely

carries canary broken glass approved they say all otherwise bonkers loose broke go for undone among the hurt

the injured the barrier bartered best not to much tamper

too much tantrums born from such balance of powers

acumen portability profitability legibility play a role so

much depends upon dependability credibility curability

a shoulder to   otherwise

otherwise

shadow in tremulous undertow

dogged   blur ridden   drawn upon

                    shared

                    spread across

            the sluiced recognizable

                    light rider

                          surface smuggler

                                smudge maestro

blousy drawl zither ramp

            tumbleless throttle flush

            whish wrangle wrung

back batter

flute-pour marl susurr

fling upon

splay

anchors away

"A shadow is simply light which has lost some of its brightness through the resistance of an object and so appears shaded." Kurt Badt

shadow as squandered light

as

remains

in the pith of translucence

aperture   reflectivit(ies)y

   where in the

   shine

   is

   volume

      [Seduction Volitional & Freedom in Emily

      Dickinson's Alcohol Poems

      [harboring no remorse the natives repaired their

      garments

   where in translucence

   is

   residency

can voluptuosity caretake extremities

the far side of extreme is closed

to visitors

where in the

shadow

is

eminence

from the scowl of a broken algorithm

      dehiscence   ledger leak

          fault line

a bleached orthodoxy wafts ~   ~   ~   ~

  ~   ~   ~

  ~   ~

breathless

indisputable

how much of

exegesis

is

privilege

shadow intransigence deputizes askew

appointment disarray   purblind   convulse concave

      concatenate crawl   creepsurfacesli p

soundless the matter yet large of bass

      correlative groom

a shape wobbly but for consideration

in the un-

established

the lurk

arrays

how much of

present

is

presence

the way

to —

ward

is

way —

ward

be-Wilder

surrey-ing the road to lost

road, bounding perplexity potholes, in the

rush of vexative disarray on the heels of a prosperous

meander,

the pause to ponder: to roam the electrical currency of

epoxy garlic, to calculate the unravellings necessary to

qualify as an effective passing lane, the burden of proof

lies with the definition, roasting through the perils of

combinatorial seepage a pledge is born, — to spend

a lifetime rummaging foam

be-Wilder (take 2)

trespass reckless   care-less

      forlorn leeches morbidity

ogive collapse ……………..

………….. counting creates

measure, you can

count on it, censorial

consort

the animal grasps

none of this

be-Wilder (take 3)

sludge come duly

scrawl calamities bituminize

penning animals as penmanship

lamentations lap the labyrinth

detritus accumulates

where in the

upset

is

circumstance

\>\>

the wild is the utterance that

precedes erasure

\>\>

put differently there is always this to consider from another point of view the early bird catches the wort worth wamble ward so it seems that is to explain this further one can say that given the circumstances accordingly as a highest priority this would rank with a high risk area in other words no through traffic which in no way obligates a slow low water crossing without fault finding bonds edge lower no man is an island in this respect we may also say to show a sign of appreciation at the very least this small token the ongoing investigation a sign of the times it is recommended check-out time is the need to serve we changed the brake fluid or, to put it differently, please refrain from clapping there will be a short intermission moreover Spring arrived early this year the global crisis hence since Russia's "hypersonic" weapon system will be the best in the world within months this means that we can put this more directly by saying that

at the outset you understand you understood that was

the beginning the exordium before being scripted

signage do not remove fineries beloved moreover there

was flotsam in her hair the very spoken for the verdict

barely in upon what was largely a domestic matter wrath

his skill contained comeupperly comelively husbandry

not an exact science data streams the disorderly misman-

aged or clearly deviant sliced of repercussion thank you

for coming wish you were here as a matter of fact the ex-

was overdue even with surely when the extension surly

just suppose neither fish nor frumpery tales so disposed

take one for the road miscellaneous acquaint why not

upon whose authority surely without fanfare freeze-dyed

the pattern not far off ever astral ever comin' round

she'll be a team of them arch beauties filigree loveliest

fairest of tribe many necklaces in front of the blind spot

you leave large gratuities clearly voiding obstacles con-

tributes to the success of for the sheer pleasure of it

nothing replaces the original save the telling forestry is

not a bad habit speeches across the mainsail clear the

deck astrodome transitions are overcome with bully this

time of year he was traded last season yet to earn current

calculations can't compare to baby doll dresses in the

Summer

how much of

substance

is

un-

substantial

askew in inveterate dislodge

> lanky loose   disperse muddle melee

> > pile-up   toss-away

> > > es-trange

yank   as-sunder

the temperature of tempest

a remedial on

all fours

disjunctive disarray conjunctive concuss

shake

to

disclose

skirt dishevel disjoint decant caper

favoring odds

surrey-ing riverrun rouse garden

leech – Andromeda – lurch

       . lunch on the grass

       . meticulously tooled blush

reasons ....

.... to

go on

how much of

conquer

is

irritability

Sundays are the pits. especially during football season.
He gets all tense. If he's in the kitchen I can sense it.
his agitation. his eagerness. as if a lot depended upon
the outcome. as if it would personally impact his life.
perhaps it does. I don't know. but I do know it impacts
mine & I suffer. there goes that word again — *suffer,*
insufferable – no way to beat it, I suffer the vicissitudes
of the game. if it's going his way, kicks to my lower
parts along with loud shouts of hurrah. things go bad,
I get rock hard fists slamming into my arms. not to
mention when his hands & arms are flailing the crumbs
are flying. flaking down into my interiors. highly
*un*comfortable. insufferable. then there's the beer &
the suds. spilling. soaking. upsetting my upholstery.
wet. soggy. miserable.

mornings like this I want to be elsewhere. what am I but a crumb-doused blue armchair reeking of beer & deposits of overbearing flatulence. a fetid chunk of disregard. yeah, the slob fell asleep after the football game & didn't rouse until after midnight. luckily it's a workday & I'll have time to recover. perhaps the pain wouldn't be so severe if I didn't have a comparison. my former home before this torture was with a quiet, elderly couple meticulous in their habits. I was always clean, my cushions fluffed. hardly ever sat in. & I was spoken of. often. in the most flattering terms. I felt cared for, . . . desirable. but they moved to a retirement home, moved me to the Salvation Army where fatso moved me here. dreaming of elsewhere is difficult. especially when I have no idea where that elsewhere would be.

askew in the frame of night

warbler

guise   currency   conspicuity curious

in undress   long seasons

biblical   ululates along the way

                    the outlook

          over-

          ripe

conveyances merely, or an

approach,

a form

of

ask

this morning I awoke feeling contradictory, — not in a white sock/brown sock kind of way, mind you, but more in a having to do with self-worth kind of way . . . a feeling of dissatisfaction with myself I feel it fair to say, sort of like, how shall I put this, . . . okay, I'll just put it, — I felt *uncomfortable.* this may seem like a small thing, a not very big deal to some, for, clearly, persons are feeling uncomfortable all the time, — for various reasons, such as: physical discomforts — hunger, cold, hot, crumbed — inadequate clothing, poor mattresses, embarrassments, etc., so why was my discomfort — a feeling which was by no means novel to me — at this point, at this point of awakening, so striking, so 'contra-dictory' as I braved to put it? because, as I see it, & please know how it pains me to share this, because, that is, my interpretation of why I was feeling 'contradictory' this morning, was because I was made, designed, put together, [assigned], for *comfort.* this metaphysical epiphany, this embrace of my place in the Great Chain

of Being, once it became clear to me where I 'stood,' so

to speak, to acknowledge the Cosmic Incompatibility of

awaking to a feeling of discomfort on the part of one de-

signed for comfort, threatened the very sense of who I

was, what I was. never mind that my cushions might go

unfluffed, that I might be littered with beer, crumbs, &

farts, these annoyances don't subvert my identity, the

cognizance of the Who that I am. a befouled Blue Arm-

chair may be a lessened version of myself, not me at my

'best,' a so called 'bad hair' day for the Blue Armchair,

but it does not deplete my telos in life, my end purpose.

you can image, then, the agony, the excruciating dis-

comfort of waking with feelings (of discomfort) in

Direct Violation of one's identity. an identity so clear &

unmistakable, built with such unambiguous, well-

defined, specificities. the wretchedness, the very sordid-

ness of betraying, of *polluting,* one of the few fine

examples today of an Immaculate Identity. the horror of collapsing that status. I can't go on like this. I just can't. If only I could mangle my structure, dissolve myself, break a leg, shatter springs, crumple into a dissatisfying heap, I would not feel so bad. I could go on. as. an uncomfortable Blue Armchair no longer uncomfortable feeling uncomfortable.

Breathing Gravity

equipoise

                        like quadruped

                        like motet

           cylindrical gasp

           balance beam

          ~

       a stir that genuflects

that considers ....

.... the cherished conjugate

unknotting

        ~

phrase in meltdown ....

.... pour

d   i   s   p   e   r   s   a   l

~

where in

gravity

is

slippage

where in

monumentality

is

distillation

~

musk

weighted

overdrawn

shy of ornamentation

suspended in

delirious

hover

~

to adduce

under the flames of a

stalled clarity

electrical helter

perceptual morose stunt

blinkered by

incognizance

a strategic cut-off

valve

the provisional

early

Monk-Like

like

lunge clump   canopy canister   ganglion frieze, chop

butterudder   back

forward

this way

that

twist turn   vertiginate

swallow   swelter

claim cluster clank crank   rustle roundabout

c   l   a   m

bustle break bother broke brother

bother bustle break brother broke

bristle

breathe

bombin-

ate   fables of late   bludgeon bark   bake

sleight slumber swell

B Flat   line periphery-burst   *stride*

intervallic surge   sully sulk skulk

         atti-T!ude

feud fidelity

     ferm   en

       ta   tion

     in-

     stall

     un-

     install

brood like ambidextrous void

roiled incongruities roll out

                a

slash-conspiracy dismembers

                a

hover strains,

                the

unsightly wedge barely

                markings

fail their indication

             — respite under the sun —

                perplexity

a subject for predication

                thresholds

volume

soluble

in the pith of brood

a murmur fumbling

an aspiration hollowed

voided

of spike

those deliberations, the ones

that fed upon miracle,

now pitted

emptied of

suggestion,

& you, all

along, moving ………..

………………………

bulk-

less

in the pith of writhe

angularity   torque

                                        , persuasion

a turbulence stymied,

                              , warded,

a fluster commotioning

rutted rampage

pitted

virulent

stab

bing

    when acrobatics

grow stale there is

always …

however

barely saw me, I wasn't there, the

move did her good, did her well, oh my

god, I've got to take a nap

don't get

morbid, the

elevator

is

to

your

right

brood askew

> leery of

assignment

> leafy with

> a

drained

wisdom,

> inveterate

underlyer teems a spent calculus

> a

stalled filtration

> a

reiterant

sedimentation

how much of

love

is

immersion

where in the

shadow

is

undertow

Ephesus Glom Part Two: An Interview with Heller Levinson and Linda Lynch by Jonathan Mulcahy-King was originally published in the February 2018 issue of *X-Peri*.

https://x-peri.blogspot.com/2018/02/ephesus-glom-part-two-interview-with.html

The uniqueness of Hinging—as a post-language innovation can be found in its unwavering study of the term (a given word) through its "application". In doing so, the hingist approaches a term as an archeologist might a fossil or artefact—it is dug up, analyzed, chipped away at, an inventory is made, it is carbon-dated and processed for vital information, a representation is made to project its innate potential etc. In this sense, Hinge does for the word what BpNichol did for the letter (See "H: An Excursion" bpNichol Archive), it poeticizes and re-presents language as a chain of information, moving reflexively as it navigates through the "beautiful quixotic". This is unique as Hinge is attempting a full-scale poetic study of the term, and as a starting point, this is certainly intriguing, producing poems/applications based around the terms "askew," "seepage," "pathos," "glide," "meander", for example, means language is actually Hinging with itself, and the Hingist, is merely an observer, a scientist.

Jonathan: Heller, how do you choose a term/word to applicate? Could you describe your selection process?

Heller: First off, I wish to congratulate you on a stunning depiction (above) of how Hinge functions. Your insights are enlightening me as well. Now, your question: "How do you choose a term to applicate?" is a critical question because it serves to reveal Hinge Spirit by declaring I do not choose the term, the term chooses me. Any humility that might be attributed to me arises from the fact that I have very little (aside from being available) to do with the process. I see myself as a Hinge carrier pigeon. We have a sterling example of how a term materializes from our former interview: "As you know, Hinge insists upon the ongoing & extensive. "Ongoing" does Not refer to a sequence, or from a start to a finish (A future exploration of the term "glide" beckons), but more in the manner of leaping, associating, ... Fecundating Rotational Clusters." There you go then. Concurrent with this interview I am, to borrow your term, 'archaeologizing' "glide." Viewing the above, what would be appositional to a sequence, a step by step? A "glide" would. Instead of the "walk," the "skateboard." Exploring "glide," I turn to my former applications for source material, i.e., "tenebraed to mermaid" arises as a likely candidate, for I visualize mermaids as being rich in glide & the line "two-world strider slippering through wave-lap" morphs (properties of 'importation' &

'mutation' discussed in *tenebraed* & *Wrack Lariat*) into (still under construction, now just a working line) "stride slipper wave-lap plasmic guttural swirl." The imports exemplify how the language is always in motion, always lusting to reproduce & to selectively off-spring. Will "tenebraed to trespass" reveal fresh information? "tenebraed to step?" "querying oscillative from collapsible cordon?" This is how I pursue the quarry. Relentless seeking to embolden.

Jonathan: How much of "glide" relies on "glide", as it seems, mechanically speaking, glide might also rely on "phonemic impulsivity", albeit one of extemporaneity (which is itself a form of "glide"), and glide of course is both the consequence and the action of momentum. As an analogy, we might imagine a hang-glider maneuvering abruptly, being propelled into a new slipstream, the maneuver is not glide, but is steering, no matter how impulsive and ineffective.

Heller: It was not my intention to suggest that "the Hinge relies on glide" nor do I wish to attach any attribute to Hinge. I may wax lyrical about Hinge singing it is 'whirly not burly, loopy not droopy,' but that is different than encumbering a flux with a role or a reliance. I merely wanted to answer your question as to how a term is chosen. 'Glide' emerges as a term more in keeping with our trajectory than 'series' or 'sequence.' The terms you've introduced – impulsivity, extemporaneity, phonemic impulse, the action of momentum – are all apt.

Jonathan: So to encumber a flux with a role or reliance is against the principals of Hinge. I see how this is in keeping with the liminality and motion of language. Relatedly then, there is noticeably more of a narrative earlier in your Hinge work than in your most recent work, which is weighted more heavily toward phonemic connection/construction, would you say that's accurate, and was this a conscious decision?

Heller: As I pointed out in Part 1, my attention has been drawn more & more toward the Linguistically Undocumented, those 'terms' currently deprived of sufficient recognition. For a narrative-oriented work such as "from Buffalo this Indian," I had available over seven books to study (see *Wrack Lariat*, p.163). To pursue a poetic dissection/exploration of the term askew, where would you turn? I searched Amazon for books on askew & the first that came up was *The American Church Experience: A Concise History*. With little material to go on, I was compelled to turn to applications arising from my own most recent publication, tenebraed: "tenebraed to disarray;" "tenebraed to disparity;" "tenebraed to tangle" (to cite a few). Wouldn't you love to see a book devoted to examining "askew" in all its shades & perambulations?

Now permit me to reverse the role of the interviewee & play the interviewer: Could you visualize a methodical multi-pronged & extensive investigation of "askew" constituting a narrative? If so, how would it look?

Jonathan: By narrative I am of course referencing your "flute carved from the wing bone of a red-crowned crane" (*Wrack Lariat*) which is, admittedly, less about fishing & exploring, "UnCovering", as you put it, and more about a series of thematic connections (which as discussed in Part One, can be found in a YouTube video of you reading and contextualising this material from *Wrack Lariat*). But to answer your question head-on, yes, as someone drawn to hinging, I would say that if askew were a word I had discovered uncreatively (from an archive based on pattern and context), I could visualize a methodical multi-pronged & extensive investigation whereby narrative-forming would be intrinsic. The example I will give comes from a recent project I have embarked upon whereby I am interviewing various subjects about key moments in their lives. The project is predicated by a fascination I have of how we experience "new identity", especially linguistically. The idea is to intersperse the interviews to create a portrait of a group life, whereby the experience of new identity becomes the narrative, the story, and the agent. The idea is to explore personhood through poetry practice and what it means in a posthuman innovative environment. It is about new identity of poetry as well and will incorporate techniques from innovate and realist schools, but Hinge, I believe, will be a vital component. I want to explore how remarkably brave people are empowered through their language. So far I have three subjects, one of whom is an 85 year old lady who recently came out as queer, though has never acted on her desires, who was awarded an MBE from the Queen of England for her career as a nurse, who attended the final weeks of the last woman to be executed in Britain (in 1955 she was hung for the unremorseful shooting of a war hero and successful businessman with whom she had been in an abusive relationship, scandalized for having had multiple abortions, working at a London club as a hostess, being sexually involved with a string of married men). And, my subject is from an especially impoverished area of the city I live in, an area recently labelled the "sex work capital" of the UK. You can see from the above how Hinge is already at play, the linguistic possibilities to be uncovered. Also, my subjects are not sought out, rather they "present" by way of friends, friends of friends, colleagues etc. I do not introduce the project I have in mind, merely assess the possibility of linguistic "Hinges" that will compliment by New Identity narrative, which I should point out is less about identity politics than you may think, I would actually call this "counter-political".

If, in light of the above, I came across the term or idea of "askew" in one or more of the transcripts and were able to map its significance and growth as a linguistic ingredient of New Identity, I would of course be exploring it, 'archaeologising' it, tinkering with it, and let it lead for a while, so it would become part of the narrative.

I hope this answers your question, Heller?

Heller: This is most interesting as, if I understand you correctly, you would be emplo(y)(r)ing askew to serve as an active agent among other active agents striving to establish an identity construct. My approach, on the other hand, would be to establish an identity for askew whereby it will emerge as a subject comparable to your 85 year old lady. Once "askew" has been *en-fleshened* into subject matter, it will "lead" with confidence, robustly integrating into your narrative.

This is Hinge at work: A term becoming Em-boldened &, through context-hopping, emboldening further terrain. At the same time, of course, "askew" prospers from the newly-situated fertilizations, a bi-amplification. This is how we roll along.

To deepen the exploration, I would invite long standing Hinge partner and visual artist, Linda Lynch, to weigh in. Linda, would you care to comment upon "askew," and how would you approach it from Hinging the visual?

Linda: Thank you both for this fertile conversation, which in itself is a manifestation of Hinge. I return to Heller's point of "being available." To approach *askew* is to **allow** askew. This means becoming present with the term non-directionally, allowing the term to "be" and also to ask "what is the 'idea' of askew?" and to attempt an answer, or multiple answers, with the least amount of imposition.

For me, it is about locating – not creating – but locating a point of visual connection with the term. This is where not only being available comes to bear but stepping aside is required to allow rumination of the term, or application, to find its visual connection. My role becomes that of receptor, or neuron, simply conveying natural links. In this way the works find each other, and then we see and learn after the fact what they reveal in their own dynamic by coming together.

My particular approach to drawing is non-linear from the standpoint of it not being something that occurs necessarily as one event leading logically to another. It is not narrative nor does it illustrate anything other than the history of its own making, though like language under the auspices of Hinge, it can employ "visual terms" to break open fecund ground. In this way my visual process becomes a natural and fluid tributary of Hinge.

But then we find that Hinge applies indiscriminately to any medium, allowing for everything to be elementally released from unnatural limitations. Life is non-linear, occurring facet upon facet simultaneously rather than unfolding in neat story lines, so the desire to organize our experiences becomes a futile exercise. Why should our language and art not reflect this?

Making something new in drawing requires returning drawing to its own nature. Making something new in language requires returning it to its own nature, that which it was before the constraints of rigid meaning imposed upon it.

Linda Lynch, Little Karst Drawing, 2017

SPRAY

12 See *from stone this running* (Black Widow Press, 2011), p.244, for further commentary on the ://: symbol.

39 **escape velocity of conditioning:** the escape velocity of status quo, peer group pressure, consumerism, *et al.,* might also be questioned.

40 **in the pith of still:** "Silence is not the absence of sound: it is the presence of stillness." John Luther Adams. Is it? Where in the stillness is motion? How much of stillness is silent?

42 **in the pith of remark:** here the reader is invited to fulfill the module with their own remarks. What about 'remark' is remarkable. How much is there to comment upon. What about commentary breeds commentary. What is it about that which resists commentary which says so much.

50 **not that nots:** the activation of the negative, in this case, reacts to the theory of Dark Energy as a repulsive force opposing the attractive (gravitational) force of Dark Matter. This negative or "dark" energy is causing the universe to expand at an accelerating rate.

53 **contained:** It is worth noting how the shipping "container" has made globalization possible. Also, how pregnant the term is in elements of Cognitive Metaphor Theory. This is mentioned simply to suggest further areas for investigation, i.e., container as metaphor, container as holding in, as a housing for the contained, explore the 'condition' of the contained, to suggest just a few paths.

Is Infinity the non-containable?

69 **Giaco:** abbreviating Giacometti's name to Giaco intends to show no disrespect. Rather it sources from a lifetime of involvement & study resulting in a deep feeling of familiarity.

83 "Giacometti's Gaze" first appeared in the journal "Talisman," Issue #47 – 2019.

92 **the history of the nail clipper:** Until 1675 these small things had never received any mention. In the eighteenth century a certain Philip McKinney of Baltimore patents the first nail clippers with a spring attached: the problem is solved, the fingers can squeeze with all their strength to cut toenails, incredibly tough, and the clippers will snap back automatically.

96 **While working with Van Gogh:** (see *Wrack Lariat,* Black Widow Press, 2015), pp. 179-235.

122 **Seduction Volitional & Freedom in Emily Dickinson's Alcohol Poems p.74:** Koukoutsis, Helen. (2018). "We – Bee and I – live by the quaffing – ": Seduction and Volitional Freedom in Emily Dickinson's Alcohol Poems.

The Emily Dickinson Journal. 27. 74-93. 10.1353/ edj. 2018.0004.

151 Monk-Like = an homage to Thelonious Monk.

156,7 **barely saw me** through **to your right** emanates from found conversation.

The originator of Hinge Theory, HELLER LEVINSON lives in New York.

TITLES FROM BLACK WIDOW PRESS

TRANSLATION SERIES

A Life of Poems, Poems of a Life by Anna de Noailles. Translated by Norman R. Shapiro. Introduction by Catherine Perry.

Approximate Man and Other Writings by Tristan Tzara. Translated and edited by Mary Ann Caws.

Art Poétique by Guillevic. Translated by Maureen Smith.

The Big Game by Benjamin Péret. Translated with an introduction by Marilyn Kallet.

Boris Vian Invents Boris Vian: A Boris Vian Reader. Edited and translated by Julia Older.

Capital of Pain by Paul Eluard. Translated by Mary Ann Caws, Patricia Terry, and Nancy Kline.

Chanson Dada: Selected Poems by Tristan Tzara. Translated with an introduction and essay by Lee Harwood.

Earthlight (Clair de Terre) by André Breton. Translated by Bill Zavatsky and Zack Rogow. (New and revised edition.)

Essential Poems and Prose of Jules Laforgue. Translated and edited by Patricia Terry.

Essential Poems and Writings of Joyce Mansour: A Bilingual Anthology. Translated with an introduction by Serge Gavronsky.

Essential Poems and Writings of Robert Desnos: A Bilingual Anthology. Edited with an introduction and essay by Mary Ann Caws.

EyeSeas (Les Ziaux) by Raymond Queneau. Translated with an introduction by Daniela Hurezanu and Stephen Kessler.

Fables in a Modern Key by Pierre Coran. Translated by Norman R. Shapiro. Full-color illustrations by Olga Pastuchiv.

Fables of Town & Country by Pierre Coran. Translated by Norman R. Shapiro. Full-color illustrations by Olga Pastuchiv.

Forbidden Pleasures: New Selected Poems 1924–1949 by Luis Cernuda. Translated by Stephen Kessler.

Furor and Mystery & Other Writings by René Char. Translated by Mary Ann Caws and Nancy Kline.

The Gentle Genius of Cécile Périn: Selected Poems (1906–1956). Edited and translated by Norman R. Shapiro.

Guarding the Air: Selected Poems of Gunnar Harding. Translated and edited by Roger Greenwald.

Howls & Growls: French Poems to Bark By. Translated by Norman R. Shapiro; illustrated by Olga K. Pastuchiv. *(forthcoming)*

I Have Invented Nothing: Selected Poems by Jean-Pierre Rosnay. Translated by J. Kates.

The Inventor of Love & Other Writings by Gherasim Luca. Translated by Julian & Laura Semilian. Introduction by Andrei Codrescu. Essay by Petre Răileanu.

Jules Supervielle: Selected Prose and Poetry. Translated by Nancy Kline & Patricia Terry.

La Fontaine's Bawdy by Jean de La Fontaine. Translated with an introduction by Norman R. Shapiro.

Last Love Poems of Paul Eluard. Translated with an introduction by Marilyn Kallet.

Love, Poetry (L'amour la poésie) by Paul Eluard. Translated with an essay by Stuart Kendall.

Pierre Reverdy: Poems, Early to Late. Translated by Mary Ann Caws and Patricia Terry.

Poems of André Breton: A Bilingual Anthology. Translated with essays by Jean-Pierre Cauvin and Mary Ann Caws.

Poems of A.O. Barnabooth by Valery Larbaud. Translated by Ron Padgett and Bill Zavatsky.

Poems of Consummation by Vicente Aleixandre. Translated by Stephen Kessler.

Préversities: A Jacques Prévert Sampler. Translated and edited by Norman R. Shapiro.

RhymAmusings (AmuseRimes) by Pierre Coran. Translated by Norman R. Shapiro. *(forthcoming)*

The Sea and Other Poems by Guillevic. Translated by Patricia Terry. Introduction by Monique Chefdor.

Through Naked Branches by Tarjei Vesaas. Translated, edited, and introduced by Roger Greenwald.

To Speak, to Tell You? Poems by Sabine Sicaud. Translated by Norman R. Shapiro. Introduction and notes by Odile Ayral-Clause.

MODERN POETRY SERIES

BARNSTONE, WILLIS.
ABC of Translation
African Bestiary **(forthcoming)**

BRINKS, DAVE.
The Caveat Onus
The Secret Brain: Selected Poems 1995–2012

CESEREANU, RUXANDRA.
Crusader-Woman. Translated by Adam J. Sorkin.
    Introduction by Andrei Codrescu.
Forgiven Submarine by Ruxandra Cesereanu
    and Andrei Codrescu.

ESHLEMAN, CLAYTON.
An Alchemist with One Eye on Fire
Anticline
Archaic Design
Clayton Eshleman/The Essential Poetry: 1960–2015
Grindstone of Rapport: A Clayton Eshleman Reader
Penetralia
Pollen Aria **(forthcoming)**
The Price of Experience
Curdled Skulls: Poems of Bernard Bador. Translated
    by Bernard Bador with Clayton Eshleman.
Endure: Poems by Bei Dao. Translated by
    Clayton Eshleman and Lucas Klein.

JORIS, PIERRE.
Barzakh (Poems 2000–2012)
Exile Is My Trade: A Habib Tengour Reader

KALLET, MARILYN.
How Our Bodies Learned
The Love That Moves Me
Packing Light: New and Selected Poems
Disenchanted City (La ville désenchantée)
    by Chantal Bizzini. Translated by
    J. Bradford Anderson, Darren Jackson,
    and Marilyn Kallet.

KELLY, ROBERT.
Fire Exit
The Hexagon

KESSLER, STEPHEN.
Garage Elegies

LAVENDER, BILL.
Memory Wing

LEVINSON, HELLER.
from stone this running
LinguaQuake
Tenebraed
Un-
Wrack Lariat

OLSON, JOHN.
Backscatter: New and Selected Poems
Dada Budapest
Larynx Galaxy

OSUNDARE, NIYI.
City Without People: The Katrina Poems

ROBERTSON, MEBANE.
An American Unconscious
Signal from Draco: New and Selected Poems

ROTHENBERG, JEROME.
Concealments and Caprichos
Eye of Witness: A J. Rothenberg Reader. Edited
    with commentaries by Heriberto Yepez &
    Jerome Rothenberg.
The President of Desolation & Other Poems

SAÏD, AMINA.
The Present Tense of the World: Poems 2000–2009.
    Translated with an introduction by
    Marilyn Hacker.

SHIVANI, ANIS.
Soraya (Sonnets)

WARD, JERRY W., JR.
Fractal Song

LITERARY THEORY / BIOGRAPHY SERIES

*Barbaric Vast & Wild: A Gathering of Outside and
Subterranean Poetry (Poems for the Millennium,
vol. 5).* Editors: Jerome Rothenberg and
John Bloomberg-Rissman

Clayton Eshleman: The Whole Art
by Stuart Kendall

Revolution of the Mind: The Life of André Breton
by Mark Polizzotti

WWW.BLACKWIDOWPRESS.COM